D1263569

THE HELP AMERICA VOTE ACT OF 2002

Legislation to Modernize America's Voting Systems

Fletcher Haulley

rosen central ™

The Rosen Publishing Group, Inc., New York

Dedicated to the newest member, Hudson

Published in 2006 by The Rosen Publishing Group, Inc.
29 East 21st Street, New York, NY 10010

Library of Congress Cataloging-in-Publication Data

Haulley, Fletcher.
The Help America Vote Act of 2002: legislation to modernize America's voting systems/by Fletcher Haulley.–1st ed.
    p. cm.–(The library of American laws and legal principles)
Includes bibliographical references and index.
ISBN 1-4042-0453-9 (library binding)
1. United States. Help America Vote Act of 2002. 2. Voting-machines–Law and legislation–United States. 3. Voting–United States. I. Title. II. Series.
KF4904.H38 2006
342.73'07–dc22

2005003619

Manufactured in the United States of America

On the cover: The main entrance of the United States Supreme Court building faces the U.S. Capitol in Washington, D.C. The marble statue on the right side of the entrance represents Authority of Law and was carved by James Earle Fraser. The male figure holds a sword and a tablet, on which is written the Latin word *Lex*, meaning "law."

CONTENTS

INTRODUCTION

The idea of government has changed a great deal since the ancient Greeks were the most powerful civilization in the known world. However, ancient Greek concepts and practices live on today. The Greeks pioneered democracy. The first instance of citizens directly choosing their ruler took place in Athens, the Greek capital, around the fifth century BC.

Democracy in ancient Greece was very different from what we know today. Women were excluded from political power, and there was no political role for minorities. Moreover, ancient Greece was a civilization that practiced slavery. In fact, only men who owned land had a say in how the government operated. Although there are significant differences between this early form of democracy and modern democracy, the idea that government should be of the people, for the people, and by the people is central to both. Who the Greeks thought of as the people—or citizens, to be more precise—was an entirely different matter.

In the 2,000 years since the ancient Greek democracy, there have been hundreds of different governments, kingdoms, and republics. Kings, whose right to rule passed on to younger family members when they died or could no longer do their job, ran many of these nations. This was especially true of Europe during the 1600s. North America had been discovered about a hundred years earlier, and European rulers were just starting to learn how to take advantage of its natural wealth. (This wealth included animal furs that sold for high prices in Europe and high-quality timber that was ideal for building ships.) Europeans looking for riches or just a better life in general moved to the New World and its colonies.

As the colonies in America grew, they became more and more independent. The colonists had no voice in the British government, although they were part of the British Empire. The British government treated the colonies as mere moneymaking machines. A series of tax increases on the American settlers started to make the colonists restless. They began to question why they should pay British taxes if they weren't allowed to have a voice in the British government. They saw this reality of taxation without representation as putting them in a virtual state of servitude. It all came to an end when the colonists revolted in 1776. At the end of the American Revolution, the United States was born and democracy was established. The English colonists became Americans when they claimed their right to choose their own government.

Since the American Revolution, American democracy has been a work in progress. At first, only white men could vote, just as in many countries throughout the world at the time. As time passed, and ideas about the equality of each citizen changed, the right to vote was given to groups that previously had been left out. Black men were finally given the right to vote in 1866, and women were not given the right until 54 years later, in 1920.

Over the next eighty years, constant improvements needed to be made to the voting system. The different political parties have always argued over what conditions should be put on voting. Should people convicted of felony crimes lose their right to vote? Should the time immigrants live in the country before they become citizens be changed so that they can vote for the men and women who make the laws that govern them?

The United States was a large country in 1919, with just more than 100 million people. Since then, it has grown to be three times as large, with a population now nearing 300 million. Counting these

Titled *The First Vote*, this illustration by Alfred R. Waud celebrates the extension of voting rights to African American men during Reconstruction in the South. It was published in *Harper's Weekly* on November 16, 1867, with a caption that read, "The Freedmen are represented marching to the ballot box to deposit their first vote . . . looking serious and solemn and determined."

votes has gone from being a large task to a difficult and complicated one. Changes constantly have to be made so that elections can take place with as few glitches as possible. When breakdowns in the system occur, they can be monumental. It was exactly such a problem that arose in Florida during the 2000 presidential election that spurred the creation of the Help America Vote Act of 2002 (HAVA).

CHAPTER ONE

The 2000 Presidential Election

The 2000 presidential election in Florida was a debacle that kept getting worse. Initial problems with individual voters led to larger problems within the system, which, in turn, exposed bigger problems in the state and, later, the country. To begin with, the 2000 election was very close. Al Gore, the Democratic candidate, actually won the popular vote (which means the total number of individual votes across the country) but lost the electoral college, which actually determines who will be president. It was the first time since 1880 that a presidential candidate had won the popular vote but lost the electoral vote, and it was only the third time it had happened at all.

By the end of election day, the results of the race for president had been determined in every state but Florida. Neither Gore nor George W. Bush, the Republican candidate, had the 270 electoral votes needed to become president. Whoever won Florida would become president, so the country stood by, watching anxiously as the Florida election commission tried to figure out who had won the election. Earlier that day, news sources had proclaimed the state would go for Gore, then Bush, before finally saying that the election was too close to call. It soon became clear that it was going to take a while to figure it out.

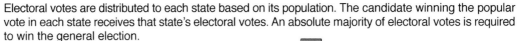

Electoral votes are distributed to each state based on its population. The candidate winning the popular vote in each state receives that state's electoral votes. An absolute majority of electoral votes is required to win the general election.

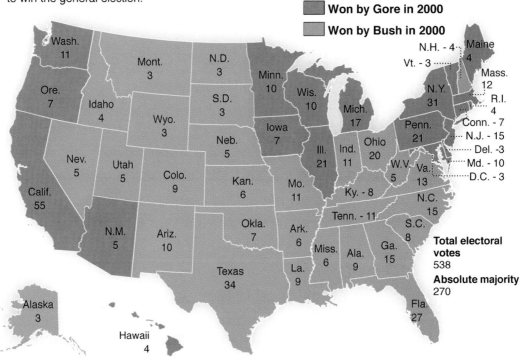

■ Won by Gore in 2000
■ Won by Bush in 2000

Wash. 11
Mont. 3
N.D. 3
Minn. 10
Wis. 10
N.H. - 4 Maine 4
Vt. - 3
Mass. 12
N.Y. 31
R.I. 4
Ore. 7
Idaho 4
S.D. 3
Mich. 17
Penn. 21
Conn. - 7
Wyo. 3
Iowa 7
N.J. - 15
Neb. 5
Ill. 21
Ind. 11
Ohio 20
Del. -3
Nev. 5
Utah 5
W.V. 5
Va. 13
Md. - 10
D.C. - 3
Colo. 9
Kan. 6
Mo. 11
Ky. - 8
Calif. 55
N.C. 15
Tenn. - 11
N.M. 5
Ariz. 10
Okla. 7
Ark. 6
S.C. 8
Miss. 6
Ala. 9
Ga. 15
Texas 34
La. 9
Alaska 3
Fla. 27
Hawaii 4

Total electoral votes 538
Absolute majority 270

This map of the United States shows the final distribution of states and their electoral college votes between George W. Bush and Al Gore for the 2000 presidential election. The reality of Gore losing the election, despite winning over a half-million votes more than Bush, revived calls for the abolition of the electoral college system.

AN ELECTORAL BREAKDOWN IN FLORIDA

The problems in Florida were numerous. It soon became obvious that not all of the votes had been counted properly. This was especially true in poorer, more heavily African American communities. It also became clear that numerous votes had been disqualified on questionable technical grounds. It appeared that partisan bias influenced some of these technical disqualifications, which increased concerns about the general fairness of the vote-counting process.

Punch Cards and Levers

Punch card machines have been widely used in Florida and throughout the rest of the United States for many decades. At one time, they were thought to be a good replacement for the outdated lever voting systems. Because elections are seldom very close, their outcomes are usually not affected by ballots that are thrown out because voters did not fully punch through the cards. However, the closeness of the 2000 presidential race in Florida placed greater significance and scrutiny on the reasons used to disqualify ballots. Eventually, the courts had to decide when these partially punched ballots, commonly referred to by the media as having "hanging chads," should be counted as legal votes.

A vote counter examines a ballot during a manual recount of Broward County, Florida, votes to determine if the intention of the voter is clear.

The lever voting machines currently being used in many states have been in service since the 1960s. However, they are based on ballot formats from the 1890s. In the late 1890s, they were praised because they were difficult to tamper with, an advantage that sustained their usage for more than a century. Today, they are widely criticized because they often malfunction and leave no paper trail in case a recount is needed.

Evidently, some officials judging whether or not a ballot was legitimate gave voters of their own political allegiance more leeway than they gave other voters. Sometimes, they even finished filling in incomplete voter forms.

A third problem was that some voters were not allowed to vote even though they were legally qualified. This resulted from the use of voter rolls that were out of date or faulty. A fourth major problem was posed by the voting machines and ballots themselves. Some of the many different machines did not work properly, and some ballots used throughout the state simply were confusing. Instead of making

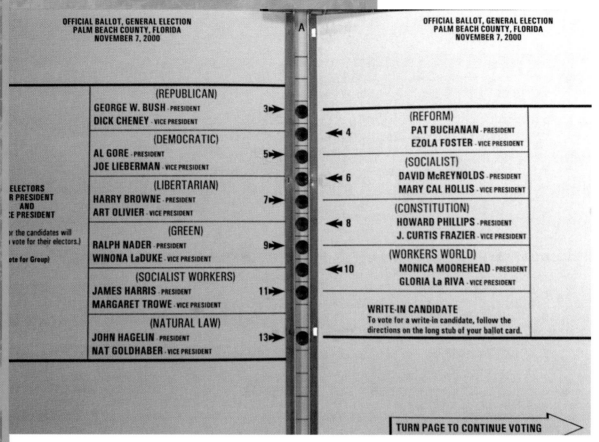

OFFICIAL BALLOT, GENERAL ELECTION
PALM BEACH COUNTY, FLORIDA
NOVEMBER 7, 2000

A

OFFICIAL BALLOT, GENERAL ELECTION
PALM BEACH COUNTY, FLORIDA
NOVEMBER 7, 2000

(REPUBLICAN)
GEORGE W. BUSH - PRESIDENT   3▶
DICK CHENEY - VICE PRESIDENT

(DEMOCRATIC)
AL GORE - PRESIDENT   5▶
JOE LIEBERMAN - VICE PRESIDENT

ELECTORS
R PRESIDENT
AND
E PRESIDENT

r the candidates will
vote for their electors.)

te for Group)

(LIBERTARIAN)
HARRY BROWNE - PRESIDENT   7▶
ART OLIVIER - VICE PRESIDENT

(GREEN)
RALPH NADER - PRESIDENT   9▶
WINONA LaDUKE - VICE PRESIDENT

(SOCIALIST WORKERS)
JAMES HARRIS - PRESIDENT   11▶
MARGARET TROWE - VICE PRESIDENT

(NATURAL LAW)
JOHN HAGELIN - PRESIDENT   13▶
NAT GOLDHABER - VICE PRESIDENT

◀ 4   (REFORM)
       PAT BUCHANAN - PRESIDENT
       EZOLA FOSTER - VICE PRESIDENT

◀ 6   (SOCIALIST)
       DAVID McREYNOLDS - PRESIDENT
       MARY CAL HOLLIS - VICE PRESIDENT

◀ 8   (CONSTITUTION)
       HOWARD PHILLIPS - PRESIDENT
       J. CURTIS FRAZIER - VICE PRESIDENT

◀ 10   (WORKERS WORLD)
       MONICA MOOREHEAD - PRESIDENT
       GLORIA La RIVA - VICE PRESIDENT

WRITE-IN CANDIDATE
To vote for a write-in candidate, follow the
directions on the long stub of your ballot card.

TURN PAGE TO CONTINUE VOTING ▶

This is the butterfly ballot that was used in Palm Beach County, Florida, during the 2000 presidential election. Many voters reported being confused about whether to punch 4 or 5 to vote for Al Gore. Although there were only 304 registered Reform Party voters in Palm Beach County, there were officially 3,407 votes for Reform candidate Pat Buchanan. Many people, including Buchanan, believed that most of these votes were intended for Gore.

clear marks indicating which candidate the voter had selected, the machines or voters themselves only made partial marks, causing uncertainty as to who was the intended choice. Also, many voters complained that the confusing placement of the punch holes on their ballots may have caused them to vote for the "wrong" person.

Perhaps one of the most infamous controversies of the Florida 2000 election was the butterfly ballot. It was a ballot that was designed to be simple and straightforward, yet like many things that happened in Florida on November 2, 2000, it accomplished

Florida secretary of state Katherine Harris and Commissioner of the Elections Division Clay Roberts certify the state's votes in the Florida capitol on November 26, 2000. They declared George Bush the winner by just 537 votes. Harris came under intense criticism, especially from Democrats, for certifying the election before all the recounts were completed. Also, since Harris had campaigned for Bush, many thought she should not be involved in certifying Florida's election results. They called for an impartial, or neutral, person to take over the certification. However, Harris refused to recuse herself.

the complete opposite. There is convincing evidence that hundreds of voters, if not thousands, accidentally voted for independent candidate Pat Buchanan when they meant to vote for Al Gore. At the end of it all, the state of voting in Florida was terrible. Many people who should have been able to vote had not been allowed to. For those who voted, there seemed to be no guarantee that their votes would even count.

THE SEARCH FOR A SOLUTION

The problems became more complicated as state officials moved to resolve them. Jeb Bush, the governor of Florida, was George W. Bush's brother and a Republican. His secretary of state, Katherine Harris, was also a Republican and had campaigned for Bush. The

Supporters of Al Gore and George Bush rally in front of the U.S. Supreme Court building on December 11, 2002, before the lawyers for the presidential candidates presented their arguments to the Court. The landmark legal battle was to determine whether the continuation of the vote recount ordered by the Florida Supreme Court was constitutional.

burden of solving the problem fell on the shoulders of Ms. Harris, who was the only one in the state who could certify the votes (which means establishing that the number of votes is correct). On Sunday, November 12, five days after the election, election officials in several Florida counties voted to conduct a manual recount of their ballots. Harris gave them until 5:00 PM the following Tuesday to submit their amended results. When the deadline passed, Harris issued new vote totals, showing Bush ahead of Gore by 537 votes, even though the recounts were not completed. If it stood, it would mean that Bush would be the next president.

Many people were dissatisfied with Harris's decisions, and several counties, joined by lawyers for Gore, sued the secretary of state to force her to allow the recounts. Gore's supporters wanted further recounting that would include all of the affected counties, or even the entire state. The Democrats took their case to the Florida Supreme Court, which ruled that Harris had to allow the extensive recounting to be completed. On November 26, Harris certified the votes anyway. Meanwhile, the Republicans had appealed to the U.S. Supreme Court for a ruling. Unlike the Florida Supreme Court, which is controlled by Democrats, Republicans control the U.S. Supreme Court. The Court ruled that any continued recounting was illegal. It argued that because each individual county had different criteria for recounting, upholding the Florida court's ruling would have infringed on the individual counties' rights.

The legal fight after the election was as political and dirty as it could get. Democrats felt that the U.S. Supreme Court was simply choosing the candidate it wanted to win when it finally administered its judgment. They also felt that the Court did not respect the rights of states to administer their own laws concerning elections. Republicans believed that Democrats were criticizing the ruling only because their candidate had lost and that the first recount that Katherine Harris allowed had answered all of the questions about the Florida votes. The problems in Florida left a terrible stain on the

Vice President Al Gore concedes the election to George W. Bush during a speech at the Old Executive Office Building in Washington, D.C., on December 13, 2000, one day after the U.S. Supreme Court ruled against his demand for a hand recount of disputed ballots in Florida. Looking on are Gore's running mate, Joe Lieberman *(front left)*, Gore's wife, Tipper *(front center)*, Lieberman's wife, Hadassah *(front right)*, and other members of the Gore family. During his address, Gore promised to work with Bush to "heal the divisions" of their bitter, drawn-out election battle.

role of the courts and the democratic process itself. One of the liberal judges on the U.S. Supreme Court issued a minority opinion (which means the opinion of the losing side) that said the "identity of the loser is perfectly clear. It is the nation's confidence in the judge as an impartial guardian of the rule of law."

CHAPTER TWO

The Beginnings of Election Reform

Florida's 2000 election was a disaster that could have happened in just about any state. For a nation that prides itself on being a symbol of democracy to the rest of the world, there are many aspects of the election process that can erode voter confidence. In nearly every election, there are problems that are simply not widely reported because they don't affect the outcome of the election. Even in 2000, several other states reported having similar problems to Florida's. However, because the number of votes for each candidate was not close, the problems never became a major issue. Nevertheless, as many as 4 million votes were not counted across the country. Although the developments in Florida led to the changes, the Help America Vote Act was actually a response to voting problems that had always been around.

After the fiasco in 2000, everyone realized that changes needed to be made before the next presidential election in 2004. Some people hoped that reforms would be in place before the midterm elections in 2002. Some issues were obvious. A lot of the problems in Florida stemmed from outdated machinery that malfunctioned or from paper-based systems that were difficult to verify or recount.

These were problems that many voters across the country could understand. An average American

Thousands of demonstrators protest against the election results and the inauguration of George W. Bush during the inaugural parade in Washington, D.C., on January 20, 2001. As some of the signs indicate, many people felt that, with the U.S. Supreme Court's assistance, Bush had stolen the 2000 election. However, an independent recount, conducted months later by several media organizations, determined that Bush had indeed received more votes than Gore in Florida.

walked into a polling station on November 7, 2000, to find his or her name on a single paper list of eligible voters. In many places, the list was faulty. The names of eligible voters may have been excluded because of human error, and it often was very difficult to verify the information on the list or the voter's eligibility on the spot.

After signing his or her name on the list, the voter would likely enter a voting booth that looked like a contraption from a 1950s sci-fi movie. Oversized levers, knobs, and push buttons were a voter's tools, and they were often confusing and outdated.

It was clear to many U.S. representatives and senators that the voting systems needed to be updated. This meant that the federal government would have to subsidize, or help pay for, new machines for the individual states. Few people had a problem with this. The machines were old, new ones were needed, and it was only a matter of dedicating the money to fix the problem. There would be very little debate over this issue when election reform came up.

DIFFERING APPROACHES TO REFORM

Other issues would stir up classic differences between the two parties. Perhaps the most important argument going into the debate on election reform would concern voter registration. For Republicans, this issue revolved around voter fraud. Their major concern was stopping people not allowed to vote from taking part in elections. They would inevitably make strict requirements about the identification provisions of any bill that would be passed. Democrats, on the other hand, wanted as many people as possible to vote. This inclusiveness would be hard to reconcile with the Republicans' need for more security and tighter control.

There was little reason to believe that Republicans and Democrats would find an easy answer to how the federal government could fix its role in elections. After all, the U.S. Supreme Court had ruled that even individual counties' rights were above the right of

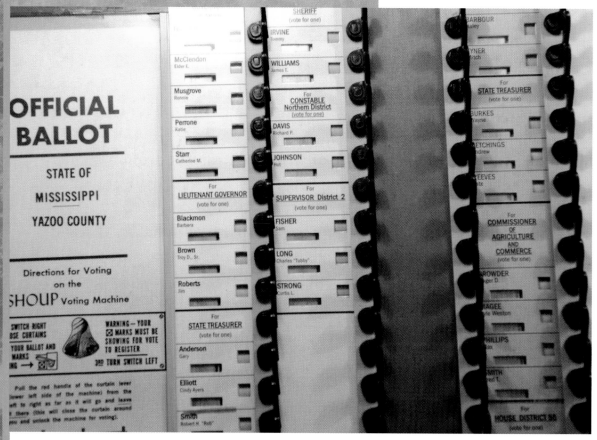

Mechanical lever machines were used by 15 to 20 percent of registered voters during the 2000 presidential election. Even before the disputed election, many states were looking for ways and funding to replace these machines, which were last manufactured in 1985.

the federal government to decide the winner of a presidential election. Elections have always been the property of local officials, so many Republican members of Congress were hesitant to change the status quo, despite the obvious problems, for fear that they would be seen as intruding on states' rights. And as could be expected, this became a significant issue when the Help America Vote Act was being debated. Democrats wanted to make federal guidelines the states would be required to follow in order to qualify for the money. Republicans saw federal guidelines as too much of a central government encroachment on states' rights.

THE FORD-CARTER COMMISSION

The first attempts to create an independent committee to study the problems that arose in the 2000 election turned into a mess. It was initially conceived of as a bipartisan (a unified effort by both parties) program, but every little detail became a political issue. The plan fell apart over a disagreement on the composition of the commission. The Republican bloc demanded that the commission have one more Republican than Democrat (in order to break any ties in voting), and the Democrats insisted that both parties be equally represented. While the nation was demanding a solution to systemic problems in the way Americans vote, Congress couldn't even agree on how these problems would be studied, much less start work on a bill that would fix them.

In July 2001, a commission was finally created. Two former presidents, Gerald Ford and Jimmy Carter, led the group. These two men's reputations gave the commission the credibility it needed after the failed first attempt to create a commission.

The National Commission on Federal Election Reform, more commonly known as the Ford-Carter Commission, made a range of recommendations that many members of Congress embraced. It suggested that states be granted money for the replacement of old and outdated voting technology. It also recommended that a limit be placed on ballot error.

The Ford-Carter Commission asked for a stipulation that necessitated no more than a 2 percent error rate. In other words, if a state used the money it was given to purchase new voting technology, the new systems would have to get at least 49 out of every 50 votes right. The number could have easily been lowered to 1 percent, which would have significantly raised the standard for the states' elections, but it was kept at 2 percent so as not to impose too much burden on the local officials. Still, by recommending any sort of minimums at all, the two former presidents opened debate

Former president Jimmy Carter addresses members of the media during a White House ceremony to release the report of the Ford-Carter Commission on July 31, 2001, as president Bush looks on. Titled "To Ensure Pride and Confidence in the Electoral Process," the report recommended many voting reforms, including making Election Day a national holiday.

on whether the federal government should hold the states responsible for the money they would be given.

The Ford-Carter Commission also made some more ambitious recommendations to reform the elections process. For example, it urged making Election Day a national holiday to encourage people to vote. The commission also suggested pushing major television networks to provide free airtime as elections neared to excite voters. Lawmakers in Washington took neither of these suggestions very seriously.

AN ELECTION REFORM LAW IS PROPOSED

In December 2001, representatives Bob Ney, a Republican from Ohio, and Steny Hoyer, a Democrat from Maryland, introduced a bill into the House of Representatives. The proposed legislation kicked off the official debate on national election reform. More than a year had passed since the presidential election of 2000. The September 11, 2001, terrorist attacks on the World Trade Center in New York City and the Pentagon, outside Washington, D.C., reinforced the need for American security and delayed other issues from being discussed in Washington. But representatives Ney and Hoyer brought their bipartisan bill forward anyway. Often, very different bills are passed in the House and the Senate. Many political commentators saw the Ney-Hoyer bill as a watered-down version of the Ford-Carter Commission's recommendations.

In a nutshell, the Ney-Hoyer bill asked for money to fund updating voting technology and improving voter access to polls in the states, provided the states meet some very minimal standards. The bill also sought to create a federal panel that would watch election results in the future. As bill sponsor Bob Ney said, "The commission won't be making rules and regulations every day from Washington, D.C., telling local officials how to run elections." Such a bill was a victory for neither the Democrats nor Republicans. It set the agenda for the debate in the Senate. It specified which questions would be debated and eventually answered by the final bill sent to the president for his signature.

The Ney-Hoyer bill required a state to allow its voters to verify that their ballot is correct if the state received federally funded new machines. However, it did not require the state to notify voters if they had somehow done something to invalidate their ballot, or if they had missed some sections on the ballot. This was one of the major problems in Florida, where the butterfly ballot made checking the appropriate box a confusing problem.

Major Voting Acts in American History

Black American men were finally granted the right to vote after the Civil War (1861–1865). In the South, where racist attitudes remained for many decades, black men trying to vote were not fully protected by the government until the early 1960s, when further protections under the law were created. Women's right to vote was also a hard-fought battle. The fight began in 1848, led by Lucretia Mott, among others. Nationally, women weren't granted the right to vote until after the First World War, in 1920. During the rebellious 1960s, young citizens began to demand their voting rights. The war in Vietnam was the main reason for the protests, and the protesters believed that if they were old enough to be drafted into the army and sent off to war, they were old enough to have the political right to vote. President Lyndon Johnson signed the Twenty-sixth Amendment in 1971, lowering the voting age to eighteen from twenty-one.

Four women cast their first votes for president at a polling station in New York City's Lower East Side in November 1920. Several states, including Wyoming, Utah, Colorado, and Idaho, granted voting rights to women long before the Nineteenth Amendment fully enfranchised American women.

In addition, the bill did not require states that bought new machines to make sure these machines had a paper trail of each vote recorded. This was another issue in Florida, where the recount became very important. Had electronic voting machines been used, there would have been no physical remains left of the votes. There would have been no way to check the machines themselves. It did not require states to provide ballots in different languages or a minimum error rate for new machines, as the Ford-Carter Commission recommended. Another requirement of the Ney-Hoyer bill was for states to create central databases of eligible voters. This database would be available to all polling officials so that eligible voters would not be turned away from voting. The bill also suggested that states have "provisional ballots" on hand, so that an individual could vote if his or her name was not on the list, and his or her eligibility could be judged later. But most important, the bill specified that $2.65 million would be given to the states for updating their voting systems. It also allowed the states to monitor their own success in using the money and following the national guidelines. Essentially, the bill was a briefcase full of cash for each state with a list of helpful recommendations.

THE DEBATE IN THE SENATE

The bill was passed by a wide margin. Three hundred sixty-two representatives voted for it, while only sixty-three voted against it. In February 2002, the debate on election reform had finally begun in the Senate. The political parties had just finished a tough fight in Congress over campaign finance reform. That bill limited the amount of money that can be donated to political campaigns and outlawed certain types of donations.

The lingering bitterness on the Democratic side over the fumbled elections also seemed to indicate that there would be another round of tough political fighting over election reform. But there turned out

Senators Mitch McConnell of Kentucky, Christopher Bond of Missouri, Chris Dodd of Connecticut, and Charles Schumer of New York *(pictured here from left to right)* celebrate the passage of a bipartisan election bill on April 11, 2002, as they go to a news conference in the Capitol. The legislation, S. 565, passed by 99 votes to 1. Senator Conrad Burns of Montana cast the only "no" vote against the bill.

to be some reforms that could be made without a major political battle. Other more contentious issues would have to be debated, and the parties were under pressure to find compromises to resolve them.

Democratic senators Charles Schumer and Robert Torricelli, along with Republican senators Mitch McConnell and Sam Brownback, introduced a new election reform bill to the Senate floor. Spirits going into the debate were much higher than a casual viewer might have expected. Ironically, Mitch McConnell, an important Senate Republican, found himself being supported by liberal watchdog groups, such as Common Cause, which had attacked him only a few weeks before during the tense campaign finance reform fight. The irony was not lost on McConnell, who joked about his new coalition, calling it "the most curious alliance since Bob Dole teamed up with Britney Spears to push Pepsi." Hopes were high as the bill was introduced. Senator Schumer told reporters that this would "consign the famous dangling chad to the dust bins of history." While it appeared going in that there would be a major fight in the Senate, the problems facing the system were simply too important to hold up the lawmaking process. However, just because the two parties had individual members willing to seek common ground on the issues didn't mean that the debate was over.

CHAPTER THREE

Getting the Final Bill Passed

Once the Senate had passed the bill, it went back into negotiations between the Senate and the House of Representatives. There were significant differences between the bills that would have to be settled before the eventual legislation could be sent to the president for final approval. The major difference between the two bills reflected the degree to which the politicians wanted to tackle the problems. While the House bill mainly tried to provide the states with money and allowed them to fix the problems themselves, the Senate bill demanded accountability and results from the states.

The Senate bill also tried to address each problem that arose on election day in 2000 in Florida specifically. It required states to allow voters to verify their ballots if they were using specific new voting machines. Also, it required states to notify voters left off the voting rolls of their right to vote on a provisional ballot.

Most important, the Senate bill had the muscle to ensure election reform. It called for the creation of a federal agency that would oversee the performance of the states. The bill created minimums for error rates in machines, allowed the agency to adopt national standards for the states to follow in the future, and gave it the power to bring civil action (which means to sue) against any state that did not comply. The

Governor Jeb Bush of Florida motions toward optical scan voting machines during a news conference in Tallahassee, Florida, on March 5, 2001. He announced the recommendations of an election reform task force, the members of which accompany him on stage, during the event. The task force suggested that the optical scan machines be used throughout the state to avoid the sort of breakdown that took place during the 2000 election.

Senate bill was an aggressive approach to election reform, and the senators believed that change would have to be forced upon the states.

The bill also added a new measure requiring new voters to provide identification the first time they voted. The identification requirement had always been a matter left up to the individual states to decide, and many states already had similar provisions in their election laws. However, making it a federal requirement would open a new debate. It was a victory for the Republicans when the requirement made it into the final Senate bill. For Republicans, it was a safeguard against voter fraud, while Democrats saw the provision as excluding Americans who did not possess driver's licenses or social security cards. These people often tend to be from poorer segments of society or immigrant communities, so it was discussed as a civil rights issue.

A compromise was reached in the final Senate bill. The provision would be included only if voters were given the right to also use their social security number or a current utility bill to prove who they are. The Senate bill also provided more money to the states than the House's original bill by about a billion dollars over five years. The Senate's version of election reform was far more ambitious than the House's. It was neither a Democratic nor a Republican victory. Certain parts of the bill, such as the identification requirements and the mandatory national standards, were bolder programs that could be claimed by each side as victories.

SETTLING THE DIFFERENCES

The negotiations between the House and the Senate did not start in earnest for several months. In September, they hit a snag that made the whole situation look perilous. The same issues that had always been expected became extremely contentious during the House-Senate discussions. This was the lawmakers' last chance to fight for their ideas before the bill was out of their hands.

Republicans stuck to their guns on the issue of preventing voter fraud. Democrats turned it into a civil rights matter, criticizing the Republicans for wanting to exclude black and Hispanic votes that usually went against them. Republicans countered by saying that the Democrats wanted to make it easier to cheat in elections. It was odd that after passing both the House and the Senate with such large margins, the eventual bill would be held up at the last step because of issues that had already been debated.

Perhaps the real reason the bill got bogged down was because the public eye had fallen off the issue of election reform. Since the

Voting by optical scan machines requires the voter to fill out a paper ballot, which the voter (or, later, an election official) inserts into a computer to be counted. Some optical scan machines, such as the one being demonstrated here by an employee of the DuPage County Board of Elections Commission in Wheaton, Illinois, print a receipt for the voter. The technology behind the system has been in use for decades in standardized testing, such as multiple choice exams, and state lotteries.

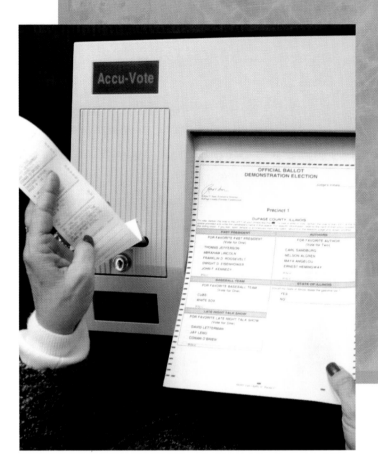

public was no longer watching, the incentive for the parties to work together was also gone. Politicians seemed to want reform only if it could gain them support in future elections.

While the impasse threatened to kill the bill, something happened in Florida that would push the federal lawmakers to make election reform a priority once again. After the 2000 election, every politician wanted to be a part of the solution. The voters who had elected them were demanding it, and many politicians knew that they could one day be involved in a disputed election, if the integrity of the electoral process was not restored. But only days after the negotiations between the Senate and the House stalled, the Florida primaries were fraught with problems. Many of the problems that marked the 2000 presidential election surfaced again, and some new ones emerged. Florida had already spent $32 million on new voting machines. State officials had purchased what the Help America Vote Act of 2002 would later suggest, Direct Recording Electronic Machines (DREs) and optical scan ballots.

These new voting technologies ended up being just as confusing as the butterfly ballots for many voters. Ballots jammed in the machines when they were counted, throwing all of the previous counts into confusion. Polling places were inexplicably closed early. Some poll workers never showed up where they were supposed to, and when they did, they were often unsure about how to operate the new systems. Some voters were even excluded from voting because the new rolls listed them as dead. Still more people were directed to the wrong polling places, where their names were not included on the local voting lists. This new failure in Florida brought the election reform issue right back onto the front pages of every major newspaper. Less than a month later, the two sides agreed on a compromise.

THE BILL BECOMES LAW

In the first week of October, the House passed the final bill. The Senate passed the bill 92–2 a week later. The only dissenting voices were the two Democratic senators from New York: Charles Schumer and Hillary Clinton. Both chose to vote against the bill because they believed that the new identification requirements would be unfairly biased against poor voters less likely to have the proper identification. The bill was passed on to President Bush on October 17 and was finally made law when he signed it on October 29.

The president had steered clear of the issue since being elected. One of the major questions during the Florida recount was how the new president would gain legitimacy. Two years after coming to power, the president was aware that there was still a large segment of the population that continued to believe that he had lost the election and was in office only because the U.S. Supreme Court had settled a court case in his favor. Therefore, President Bush sought to distance

President Bush signs the Help America Vote Act of 2002 on October 29, 2002, as several members of Congress look on. During the signing ceremony, the president described the new legislation as an important reform for the country. He also said that the law should "help states and localities update their systems of voting and ensure the integrity of elections in America."

himself from the debacle and move on with his presidency. Signing the election reform bill would inevitably be a big media day since it would put the president right back in the issue. During the televised signing ceremony for the Help America Vote Act, as the new law is called, President Bush steered clear of it all and said, "Every registered voter deserves to have confidence that the system is fair and elections are honest, that every vote is recorded and that the rules are consistently applied." The president never specifically mentioned Florida or the 2000 election. The new law came too late to affect the midterm elections due the following month, but conceivably, it would be well in place by the time of the next presidential election in 2004.

The Help America Vote Act is a combination of the House and Senate bills. However, it resembles the Senate bill more than the House bill in its ambitious approach to changing the way voting is carried out in the United States. To begin with, it mandates that provisional ballots be supplied to voters who believe they are eligible to vote but whose names do not appear on the voting rolls. It also requires states to allow voters the chance to review their ballot to make sure that their choices are correct. Both of these measures directly address the problems that arose in Florida during the 2000 election.

The new law followed the lead of the Senate bill regarding the contentious issue of requiring voters to show IDs the first time they vote. The requirement was established, but voters are allowed to also use their social security numbers in place of their social security cards or their driver's licenses. The amount of funds headed to the states is actually higher than either of the previous two bills proposed. Few members of Congress had problems with this because of the perceived value of funding updated technologies.

In terms of enforcement, the Help America Vote Act found the middle ground between the two bills. It established national requirements that the states receiving grant money had to meet, but the power to bring them to court over failures was left to the

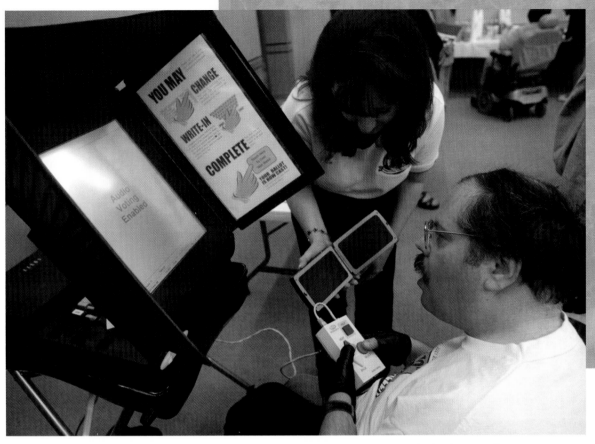

A disabled New Jersey man tests a voting machine, with some help from a Sequoia Voting Systems sales executive, at a Voting Technology Expo in North Brunswick, New Jersey, on August 7, 2003. New Jersey sponsored several of these expos across the state in an effort to equip its polling stations with accessible voting equipment for the disabled, as required by the Help America Vote Act of 2002.

attorney general's office. In the Senate bill, this power rested with the commission itself, but a little more leeway was given to the states when the final bill added another step to the enforcement process.

The legislation also provides funds for states to make their polling places more accessible to people with disabilities. This includes providing special booths at each polling place that would make the voting experience easier for disabled voters. This was one of the first issues to be raised about election reform, but since neither side opposed it, it was easily included in both the House and Senate versions of the bill.

The Help America Vote Act does not require electronic voting machines to produce a paper trail. This was one of the compromises made by the Senate in its negotiations with the House. Although the issue was conceded in the negotiations, it stayed on the table for future discussion. Ironically, it was a member of the House, Representative Rush Holt, a Democrat from New Jersey, who almost immediately began trying to find support for an amendment to the law that would require paper records of votes using these machines. As it stands, though, it is up to each state to decide if its electronic systems will produce a paper trail.

CHAPTER FOUR

What to Expect from the Help America Vote Act of 2002

The Help America Vote Act of 2002 had finally been passed, but did it go far enough? Did it guarantee that another Florida 2000 would never happen again? Probably not, but it did make some important headway in fixing the way Americans vote.

In their commission report at the beginning of this process, former presidents Gerald Ford and Jimmy Carter admitted that all of their recommendations should not be adopted right away. They argued that a complete implementation of their recommendations could cause confusion and throw upcoming elections into turmoil if the system was changed too quickly. Furthermore, there was the issue of enforcement. A bill with laws that cannot be enforced is simply not useful. There was also the issue of the voters themselves. Would voters be able to catch up with all of the changes? After all, voters don't get much practice. The average American will vote only a handful of times every four years, so adding significantly different new technologies to the process might only confuse the voter.

This is exactly what happened in Florida in 2002. Completely new voting machines were used that confused both the voters and the polling officials. If a voter finds it difficult or impossible to cast a ballot for

Optical Scans and Direct Recording Electronic Machines

The optical scan systems became favorites of the politicians addressing election reform after 2000 because they allow for votes to be counted easily and they produce a physical record of the votes. However, the technology wasn't quite ready for official use. In the Florida 2002 gubernatorial primary, the counting machines often jammed, and the polling workers weren't properly trained.

The Direct Recording Electronic Machines (DREs) have been highly recommended by the lawmakers behind the Help America Vote Act. They are well supported because they are highly efficient when being used by voters or by election officials. Like all voting systems, the DRE has its drawbacks. Its critics claim that it could be tampered with by hackers and never detected. It also does not provide a paper trail in case problems do arise.

Barbara Sanders of the League of Women Voters participates in a test of a touch-screen electronic voting machine in Columbia, Maryland, on October 13, 2004. The touch-screen technology, which has been compared to ATMs, has been criticized because it does not produce a printed record that would allow for a manual recount in close or disputed elections.

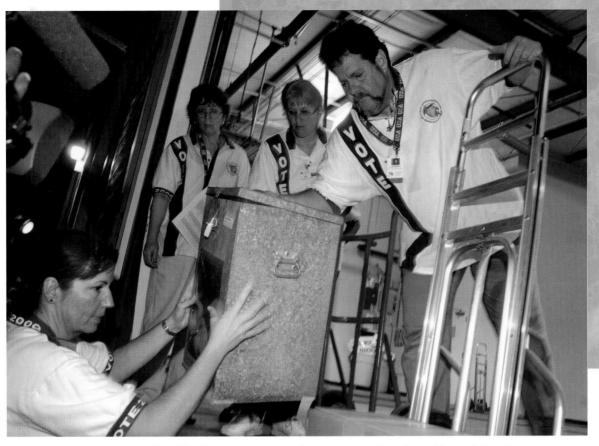

Election workers unload ballots arriving to be recounted at the office of the Orange County supervisor of elections in Orlando, Florida, on September 10, 2002. Paper ballots from 105 of Orange County's 251 precincts had to be recounted because of a design flaw.

his or her intended choice, it is just as harmful to democracy as are uncounted votes. This is perhaps the one issue that the Help America Vote Act really missed. Numerous reports released since the 2000 election have suggested that a lack of voter education programs is the biggest problem in America's election system.

There also remain some philosophical and practical questions about how ready the United States is to implement electronic voting, the favorite choice among the new technologies. Are voters ready to trust computers with counting votes? Democratic lawmakers signaled their distrust when they voted to require all of the new machines to leave a physical paper trail of each vote. But there have even been

An Ohio resident holds up a sign demanding a recount during a rally at the statehouse in Columbus, Ohio, on December 4, 2004, to draw attention to Election Day irregularities. President Bush won Ohio by a slim majority.

problems with voting systems that create physical records. In some instances, poll workers have been unable to change the roll of paper, thereby losing the paper evidence of votes.

The most important question about electronic voting is its actual efficiency. Numerous public tests have been held by the machines' manufacturers to calm voter anxiety. However, none of these tests have actually been outright successes. It seems that the states were in such a rush to improve their voting systems that they bought systems that were not quite ready for public use.

In the end, the Help America Vote Act is an important piece of legislation that addresses problems that had been ignored for years. Florida's continuing electoral shortcomings have been the impetus for this bill, but these were problems that should have been fixed long before that. It is a bill that was fairly easily passed compared

Despite their concerns about the electoral process, Americans turned out to vote in the 2004 elections. In many places, such as Fort Mill, South Carolina *(top)*, and Kaukauna, Wisconsin *(below)*, many voters were still in line after the official poll-closing time.

to other political battles going on at the time over campaign finance reform because of its nonpartisan nature. The senators and representatives deserve to be applauded for plowing through the issue even when it was no longer front-page news and for bringing a spirit of cooperation to the bargaining table.

It is important to note that the first versions of the bill were passed with great numbers. Lawmakers seriously wanted the debate to start, and they made the agreements that had to be reached in order to pass the bill and improve the voting processes in America. Some things were missed in the final bill, but as former presidents Ford and Carter noted in their first commission, sweeping changes weren't necessarily the best idea when they would affect millions of voters and fifty individual states that have always used the system that best serves their own residents.

GLOSSARY

allegiance Loyalty to a person, group, nation, or cause.

ballot The sheet of paper or card used to cast a vote.

bill A proposed law.

civil rights The social rights to which a citizen is entitled.

Congress Both the House of Representatives and Senate.

debacle A complete failure or breakdown in a system.

democracy The political system in which citizens have the right to choose their leader.

electoral college The group of people selected by each state that formally elects the president and vice president.

encroachment An intrusion into another's rights, property, or area of responsibility without permission.

federal Relating to the central government.

fiasco A significant, often sudden breakdown in a system.

legislation Written and approved law; the process of enacting laws.

liberal A person who believes it is the government's responsibility to improve social conditions and create a more equitable society.

mandatory Required.

midterm elections Elections for congressional members in the middle of a president's term.

partisan Prejudiced by support of a political party.

primaries Elections held within a political party to determine a candidate for the actual election.

provisional ballot A vote, the eligibility of which is to be determined later. A voter whose name does not appear on the voting lists is allowed to cast a provisional ballot to prevent him or her from being unfairly excluded in the event that the lists are incorrect.

ratify The act of the president signing a bill passed by Congress. When ratified, a bill becomes law.

states' rights In American politics and constitutional law, the rights of states to make laws on all issues that the U.S. Constitution does not specifically give the federal government the power to determine.

status quo The existing condition or state of affairs.

stipulation A condition or requirement in a legal document.

subsidize To aid with public money.

FOR MORE INFORMATION

Common Cause
1250 Connecticut Avenue NW, Suite 600
Washington, DC 20036
(202) 833-1200
Web site: http://www.commoncause.org

The Election Assistance Commission
1225 New York Avenue NW, Suite 1100
Washington, DC 20005
(866) 747-1471

The Federal Election Commission
999 E Street NW
Washington, DC 20463
(800) 424-9530
Web site: http://www.fec.gov

U.S. Department of Justice, Civil Rights Division
950 Pennsylvania Avenue NW
Washington, DC 20530-0001
(202) 514-2000

Web Sites

Due to the changing nature of Internet links, the Rosen Publishing Group, Inc., has developed an online list of Web sites related to the subject of this book. This site is updated regularly. Please use this link to access the list:

http://www.rosenlinks.com/lallp/hava

FOR FURTHER READING

Gottfried, Ted. *The 2000 Election*. Brookfield, CT: Milbrook Press, 2002.

Hamilton, John. *Voting in an Election* (Government in Action). Edina, MN: ABDO Publishing Company, 2005.

Landau, Elaine. *The 2000 Presidential Election*. New York, NY: Children's Press, 2002.

Sergis, Diana K. *Controversial Presidential Election Case* (Landmark Supreme Court Cases). Berkeley Heights, NJ: Enslow Publishers, 2003.

BIBLIOGRAPHY

Carter, Janelle. "Congress Sends Election Overhaul Bill to White House." Associated Press, October 17, 2002.

Carter, Jimmy, Gerald Ford, Lloyd Cutler, and Bob Michel. "Promising Proposals for Election Reform." *Washington Post*, December 3, 2001.

Cocco, Marie. "The Coming Tussle Over Voting Reform." *Record*, April 5, 2001.

"The Dodd-McConnell Bill." Retrieved October 20, 2002 (http://citizen.org/congress/govt_reform/election/dodd_mcconne).

"The Help America Vote Act." Retrieved October 22, 2002 (http://www.pbs.org/newshour/vote2004/primaries).

Holland, Judy. "Florida Chaos Boosts Voting Reform." *Times Union*, October 13, 2002.

Pear, Robert. "House and Senate Negotiators Agree on an Election Bill." *New York Times*, October 5, 2002.

Pear, Robert. "Senate Sets Aside Its Work on Overhauling Elections." *New York Times*, March 4, 2002.

Rosenbaum, David E. "House Vote Puts Overhaul of Elections Step Closer." *New York Times*, December 13, 2001.

"Senate Passes Election Overhaul Compromise." Associated Press, October 16, 2002.

Zinn, Howard. *A People's History of the United States.* New York, NY: Perennial, 2003.

INDEX

About the Author

Fletcher Haulley is a writer and researcher who lives in New York City. A graduate of New York University, he is also the author of *A Primary Source History of the Colony of New Hampshire* and the editor of *Critical Perspectives on 9/11*. Like many Americans, Haulley was gravely concerned about the electoral flaws that were highlighted during the 2000 presidential election. Accordingly, he closely followed the developments leading to the enactment of the Help America Vote Act of 2002.

Photo Credits

Cover © Royalty-Free/Corbis; pp. 6, 22 © Bettmann/Corbis; pp. 8, 18, 20, 24, 27, 29, 31, 33, 36, 37, 38, 39 © AP/Wide World Photos; p. 9 © Najlah Feanny/Corbis; pp. 10, 11, 12, 14, 16 © Reuters/Corbis.

Designer: Thomas Forget; Editor: Wayne Anderson